Brush Calligraphy

ARTHUR BAKER

Dover Publications, Inc.
New York

Published in Canada by General Publishing Company, Ltd., 30 Lesmill Road, Don Mills, Toronto, Ontario.
Published in the United Kingdom by Constable and Company, Ltd., 10 Orange Street, London WC2H 7EG.

Brush Calligraphy is a new work, first published by Dover Publications, Inc., in 1984.

DOVER *Pictorial Archive* SERIES

Manufactured in the United States of America
Dover Publications, Inc., 31 East 2nd Street, Mineola, N.Y. 11501

Library of Congress Cataloging in Publication Data
Baker, Arthur.
  Brush calligraphy.

  1. Lettering. 2. Brush drawing. I. Title.
NK3600.B25   1984   745.6′1   83-5234
ISBN 0-486-24533-0

Publisher's Note

We may thank the eruption of Vesuvius in A.D. 79 for the inspiration behind this book. In destroying Pompeii and Herculaneum, the volcano also preserved the brush-painted letters of shop signs, slogans and graffiti, letters that time and weather would have effaced had they not been covered with volcanic ash. They were painted in the style of the great epigraphic inscriptions on Roman monuments, inscriptions themselves based on the brushwork that served as a pattern for the stone carvers. But letters incised in limestone or marble lost the evidence of the brush's grace and spontaneity to the cold edge of the chisel and the multiple strokes of the hammer. It is the freedom of the brush that Arthur Baker explores in this book, which includes alphabets in the style of the classic Roman capitals, those influenced by its descendants, the adaptation of the medieval and Renaissance scribes—notably Chancery cursive—as well as semiabstract compositions that use letter elements as artistic organizing principles.

All of the alphabets included here have been executed with broad-edged brushes in various sizes, with washes and tonal variations in watercolors and gouache. Brushes have not heretofore been widely used as a primary tool in Western calligraphy, except for quick sign-painting and the like, that is, in contexts where the use of the brush has been dictated by practical rather than esthetic concerns. Both China and Japan, of course, have a long and glorious tradition of brush calligraphy, but the Asian masters use a round, sharply pointed brush, and the thickness or thinness of their lines is determined by the pressure placed on it. In brush calligraphy as practiced by Arthur Baker, by contrast, it is not so much the vertical pressure as it is the twisting of the flexible edge of the brush that creates variation in the thickness of the strokes. But Baker uses dry-brush technique and pressure on the brush as well, in creating alphabets that are not merely individual interpretations of historical hands, nor simply semiabstract compositions based on the alphabet, but a new departure for Western calligraphy, with its own panoply of methods and esthetic imperatives.

In many of the plates in this book, tonal variations—the gray of the dry brush, the translucence of watercolor—make the twisting of the brush plainly visible to the student, who is thereby provided with a way of seeing into Baker's techniques. Any flat, chisel brush—sable, camel or acrylic—can be used for brush calligraphy, with watercolor or gouache on any paper. (Note that the plates that follow have been reduced for reproduction; working in a larger size allows for greater freedom.) Arthur Baker's experiments with technique, texture and finish, as well as in letter form and alphabet composition, are a rich hoard of ideas for those who would take up the brush.

Brush
Calligraphy

EGHIJK
ORSTU
3

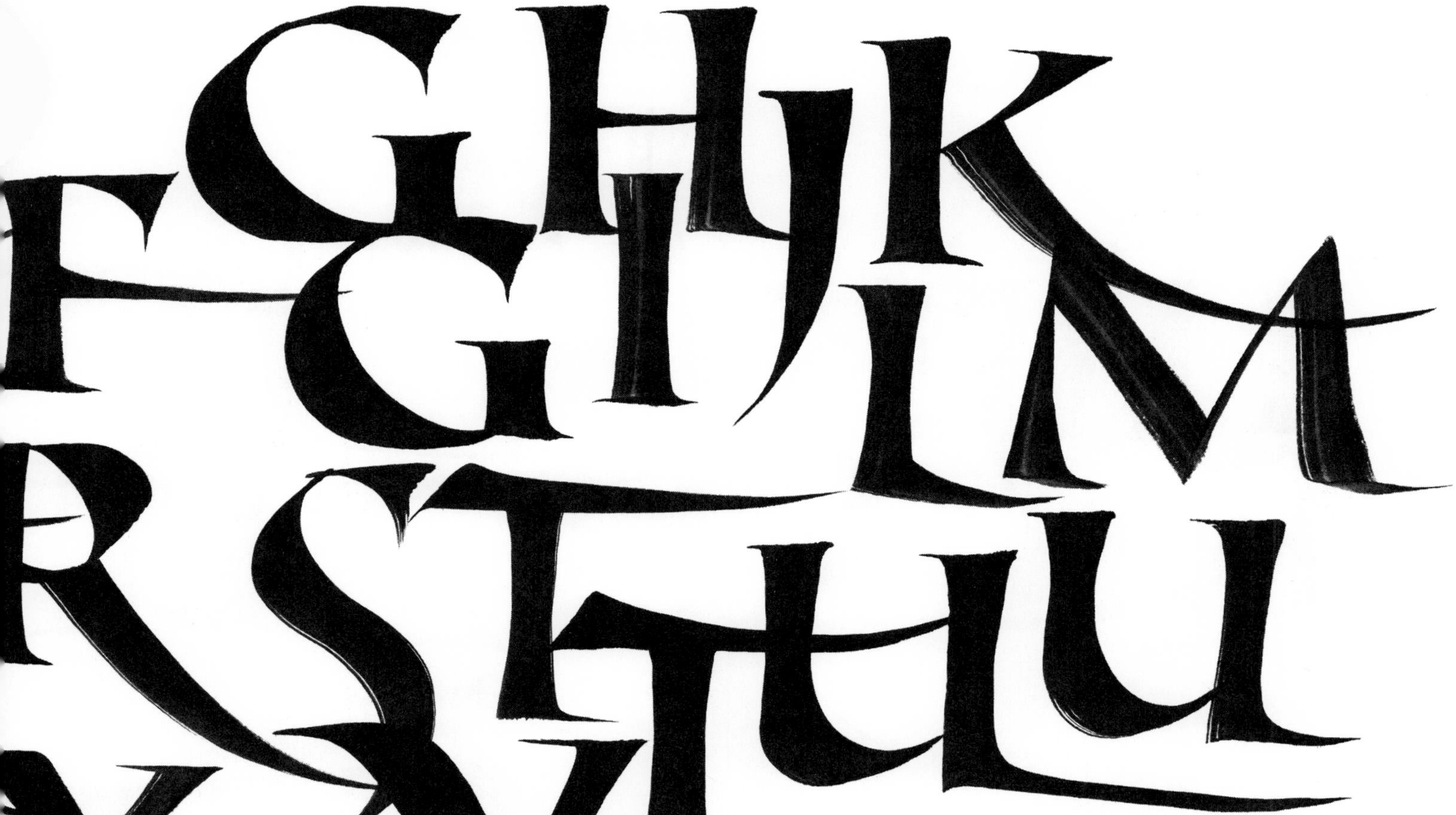

A BC BC L
HIJK R
R ST U
Z

6

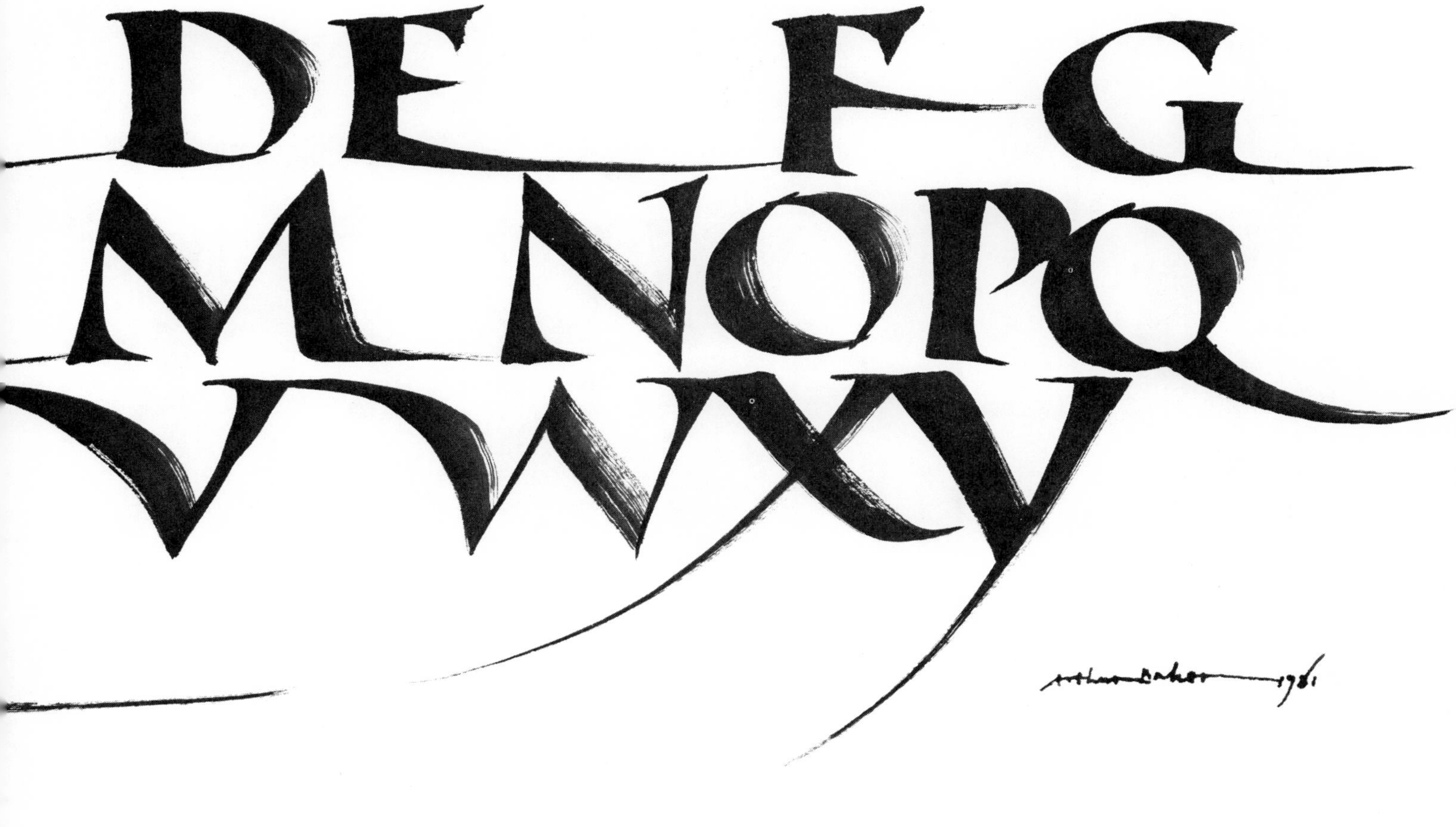
DE FG
MNOPQ
VWXY

ABC
HIJK
QRST
Z

27

arthur Baker 1981

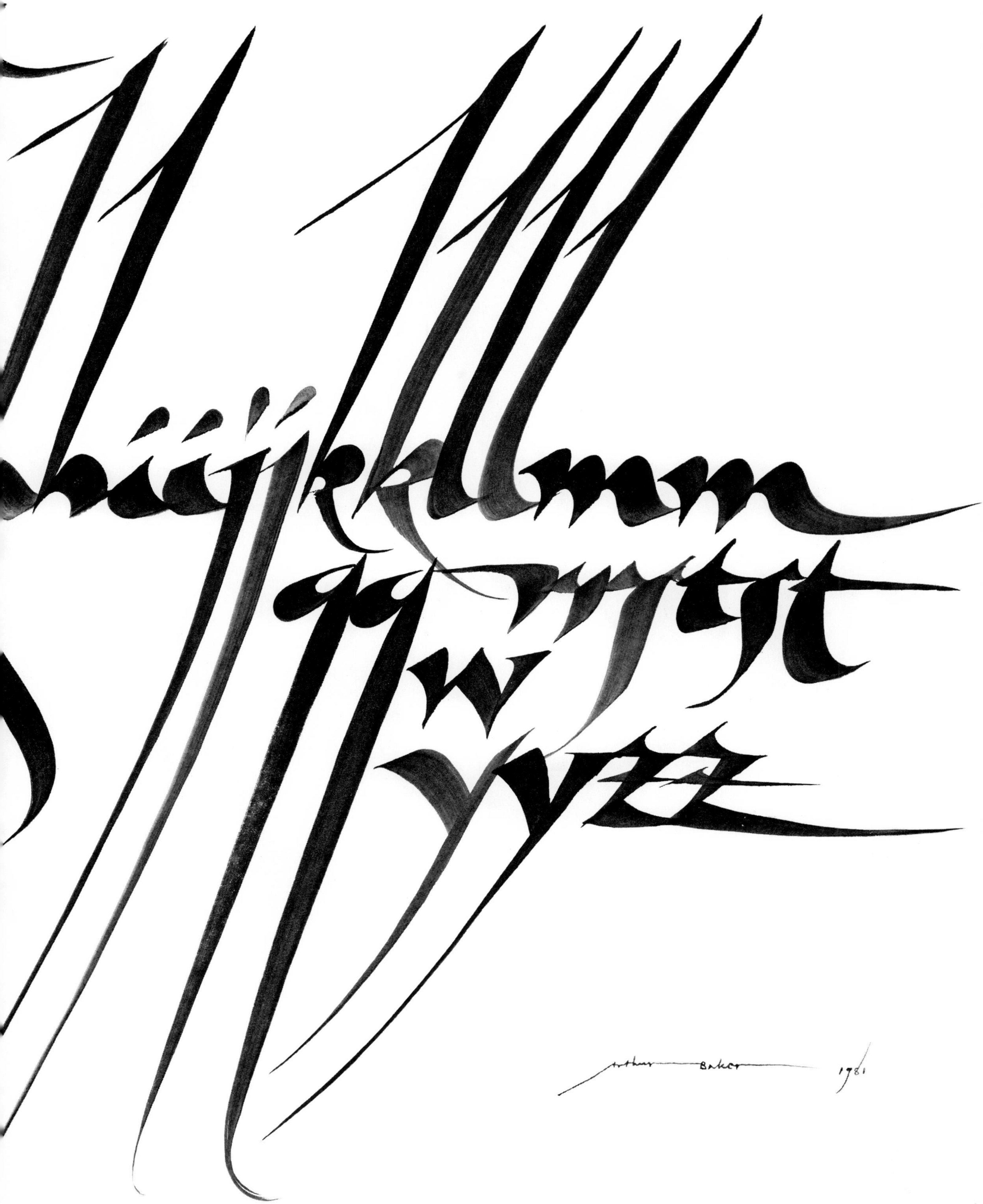

arthur baker 1981

43

arthur baker 1981

$\mathcal{M}$

mnopqrstu
xyz

arthur———Baker———1981

arthur Baker 1981

aaaabc dddde ### jk l m

54

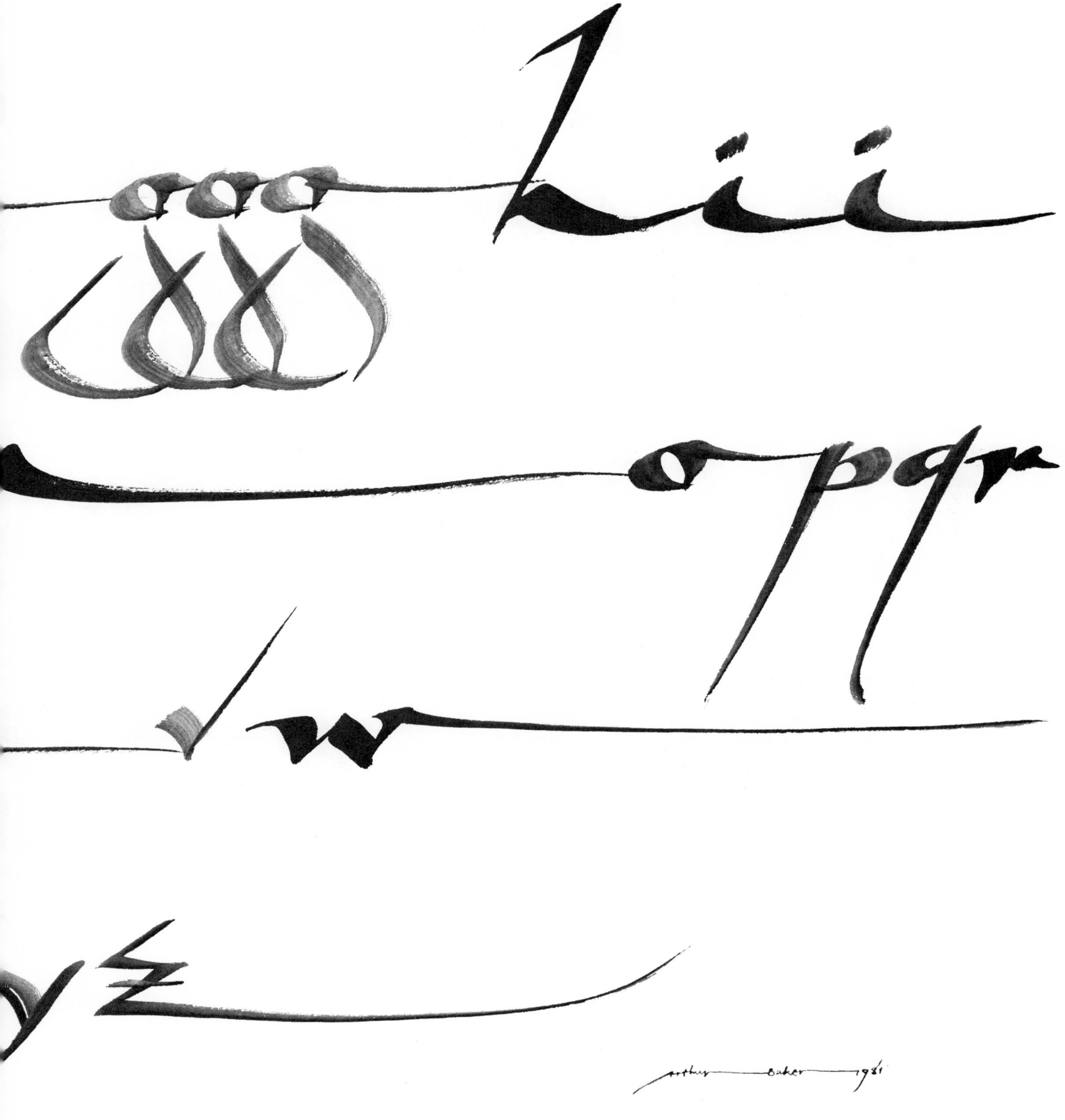
arthur baker 1981

56

arthur baker 1981

58

arthur Baker 1981

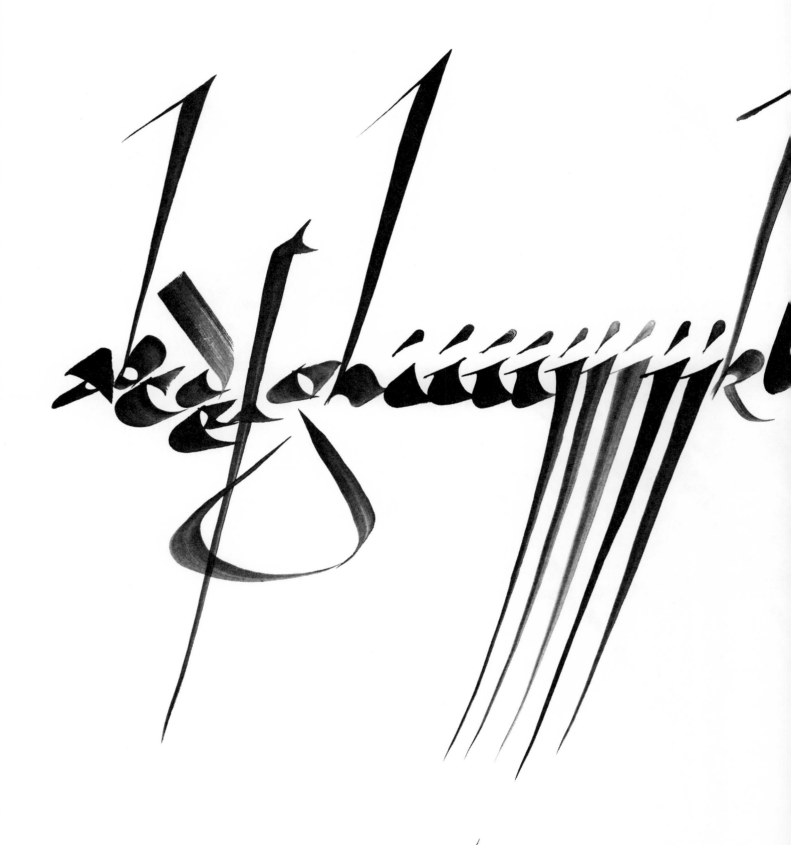

arthur Baker
1981

arthur Baker 1981

mnopqrstu

Arthur Baker 1981

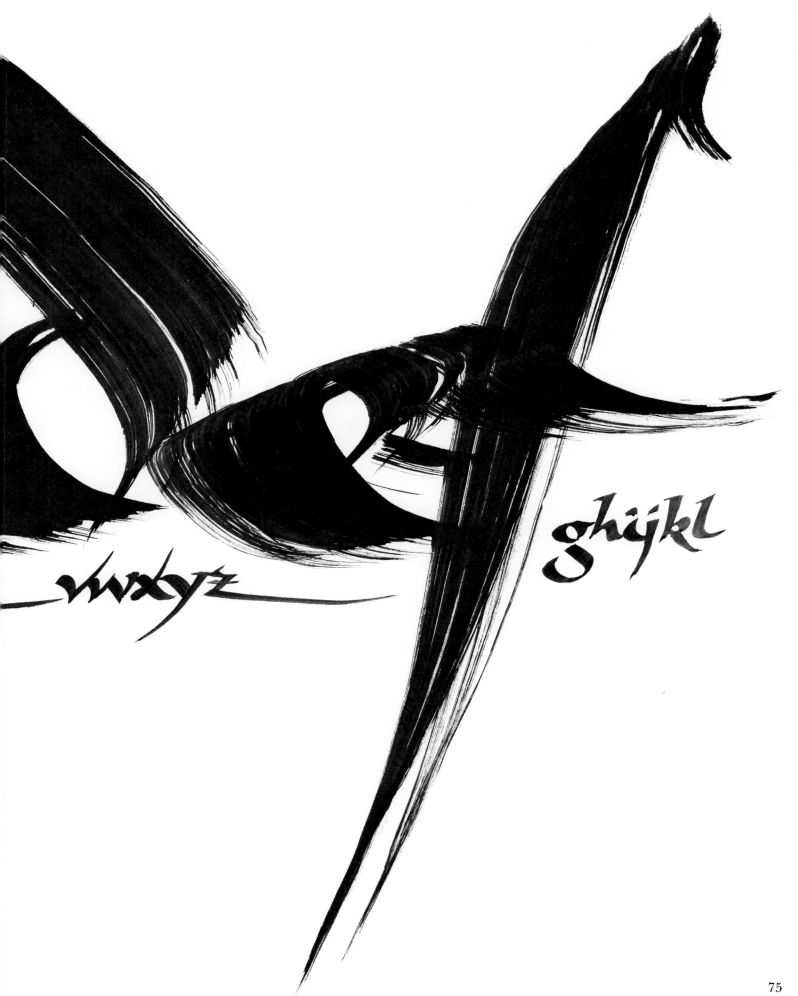

ghijkl

vwxyz

hi jkl mnopqrs
xyz

arthur baker 1981

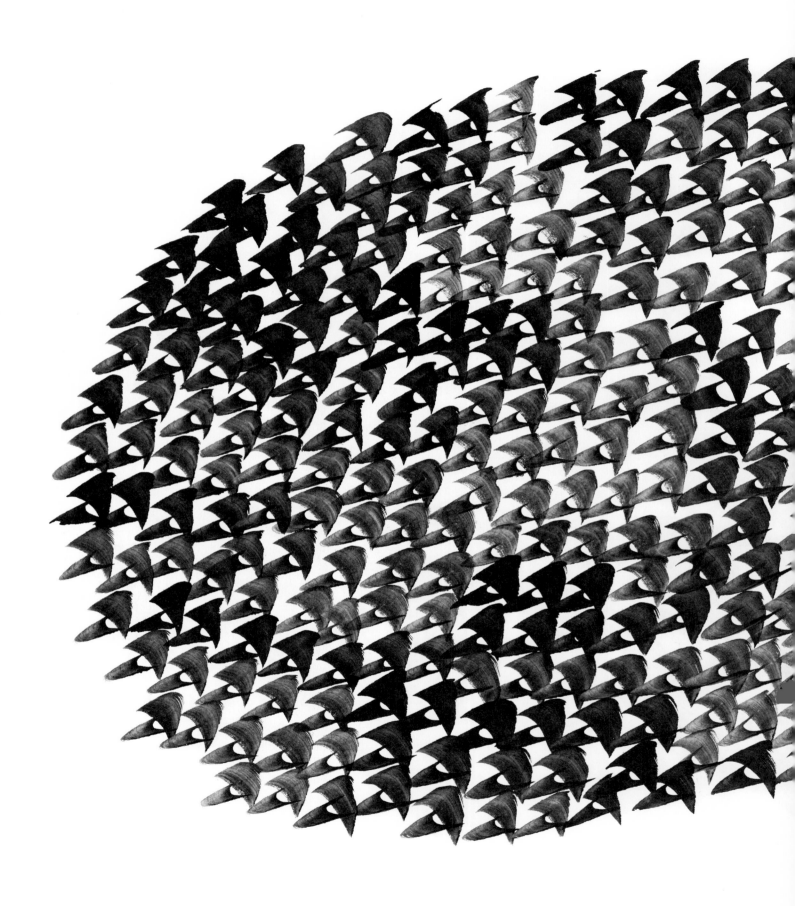

abcdefghijklmnopqrstuvwxyz

Arthur Baker 1961

ijklm nopqrst

Arthur Baker 1981

84

abcdef
ghi

Arthur Baker 1981

89